Well Earth Well Me!

Story and Photo Illustrations
by
Kenda Swartz Pepper

Eifrig Publishing LLC

Lemont   Berlin

I really love this place we call earth.

I've been playing here since the day of my birth!

I especially like the hills and the trees, the sky and the clouds, and even the breeze.

15 Tips for Parents and Kids to Help Create a Well Earth and a Well You

Hello, parents and kids. You will find lots of tips in this book to help create a well earth and a well you. If you have some tips to share or want to learn more, please do so at www.wellearthwellme.com. Together, we can make a well earth, which ultimately helps make a well you and a well WE! Wow-eee! Well done, indeed.

Well Earth
Well Me
Well Me oh My oh Me!

1. Voice Your Power

You can become an Earth Ambassador at your school by starting a Well Earth Club. Together you can pick up litter in the schoolyard, promote recycling, or even create a school garden. Children are stepping up, speaking out, and becoming leaders for making positive change. Power your voice and voice your power!

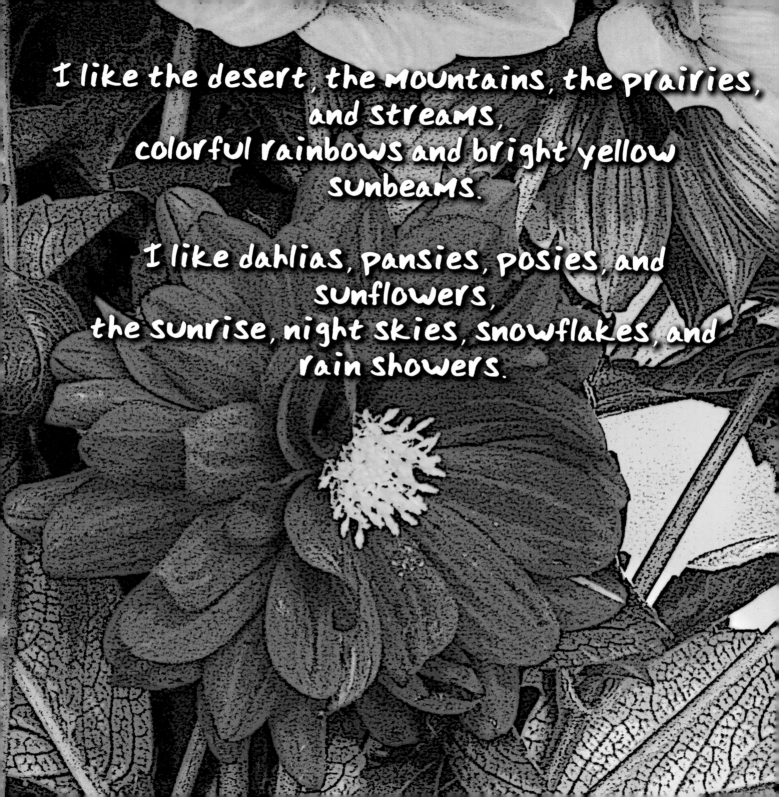

I like the desert, the mountains, the prairies, and streams,
colorful rainbows and bright yellow sunbeams.

I like dahlias, pansies, posies, and sunflowers,
the sunrise, night skies, snowflakes, and rain showers.

Well Earth
Well Me
Well Me oh My oh Me!

2. How Does Your Garden Grow?

Have you ever grown a garden? You can grow herbs, flowers, vegetables, or even a fruit tree. You can also grow your own *organic* food simply using seeds, sunshine, and water. Growing your own garden -- in your backyard, on a window sill, or even in a shared urban garden -- helps the environment too. Food you grow yourself is free of packaging and often has higher vitamin content and more flavor than food you find in the store!

Well Earth
Well Me
Well Me oh My oh Me!

3. Know Where Your H2O Goes

Did you know that you can save gallons of water a minute by turning off the faucet while you are brushing your teeth or washing your hands? If you want to see how much water you can save, try this experiment: Place a gallon container in your sink under the faucet. Turn on the water and keep it running while you brush or wash. As the container fills up, transfer the water to a bucket (find a good use for that water). You can then calculate how much water you will save each week, month, and year by simply turning off the faucet.

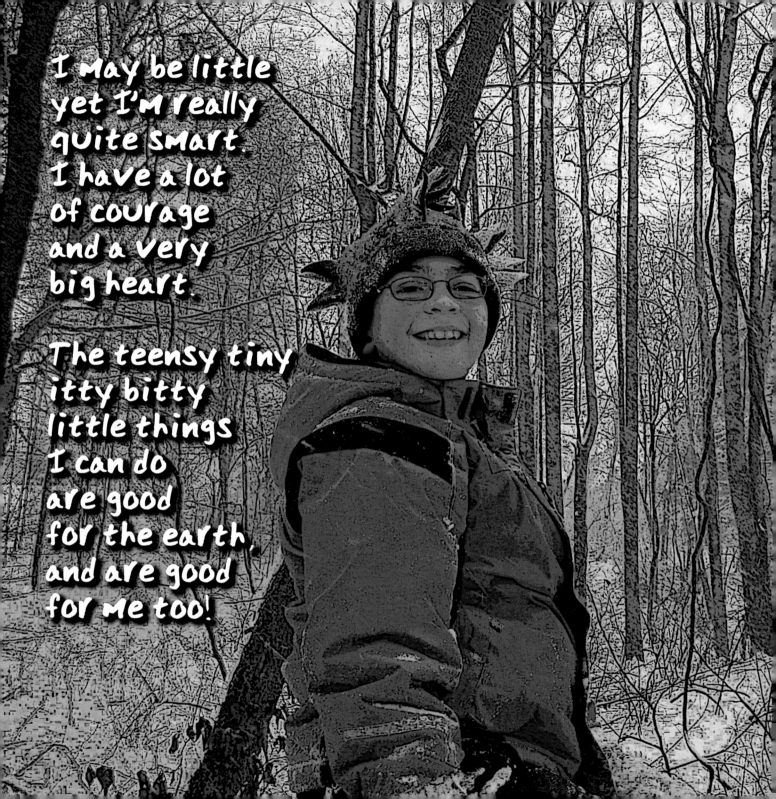

I may be little
yet I'm really
quite smart.
I have a lot
of courage
and a very
big heart.

The teensy tiny
itty bitty
little things
I can do
are good
for the earth,
and are good
for me too!

Well Earth
Well Me
Well Me oh My oh Me!

4. Kids Helping Kids Helping the Earth by Reducing, Reusing, and Recycling

A lot of unnecessary rubbish ends up in landfills: packaging, disposable containers and utensils, and many other non-degradable products. Try using containers that can be reused, especially for lunches and outings. Instead of throwing away the toys and clothes that you have outgrown, you can help the earth and other kids by donating these items to your local thrift store. And when you shop, look for products made from recycled materials, so the recycling loop can come full circle.

There are many little things that I can do
like turning off faucets and the lights too!

Even little things save water and energy.

This is good for the earth,
so that's good for me!

Well Earth
Well Me
Well Me oh My oh Me!

5. Empower Yourself to Power Down

You can reduce your electricity usage by fully turning off electronic equipment and appliances. These items are still using electricity when they are on *standby*, so you can save even more by getting a smart power strip. A smart power strip uses less electricity and automatically cuts off power to devices that are not in use. It saves your family money, saves electricity, and helps create a well earth. It's a win-win-win!

Well Earth
Well Me
Well Me oh My oh Me!

6. Keep the Trees Please

What is the best way to keep trees in the forest? Reduce your paper product usage! You can do this by using towels made of cloth rather than paper. You can buy products made from post-consumer waste, bamboo, or other sustainable materials for your household and school needs. You can even save paper by using old newspapers or magazines to wrap gifts. Use your creativity to create a well earth, and keep the trees please!

I eat vegetables that are
green and purple and orange and red.
This makes the earth colorful
and keeps my body well fed.

Well Earth
Well Me
Well Me oh My oh Me!

7. Captain Compost to the Rescue!

Did you know that yard waste such as leaves and cut grass, together with food scraps, make up more than a quarter of the U.S. solid waste in landfills? There's no need to send your yard trimmings and leftover food to the landfill when you can turn it into valuable soil fertilizer – compost! Composting is an earth-happy way to turn that waste into a rich, yummy treat for your soil. And the superhero earth-making worms LOVE it too!

Fruits of all colors like yellow and blue,
are yummy and sweet
and so good for me too!

Well Earth
Well Me
Well Me oh My
oh Me!

8. Orange You Glad You Like Oranges . . . and Pineapples and Blueberries?
How about a yummy juicy orange instead of candy? Or a crisp red apple for a snack? Or sweet delicious blueberries and oatmeal for breakfast? By eating fruit, you give your body important vitamins and a treat all at the same time! You + Fruit = A Well You!

I can plant little seeds that grow into flowers that feed honeybees and give them their powers.

The bees use those powers to pollinate more flowers!

Well Earth
Well Me
Well Me oh My oh Me!

9. Bees are People Too

Okay, bees really are not people. Bees are insects. But you knew that already! While bees are obviously not people, they do make it possible to grow the food that people eat. The earth needs bees and other pollinators to help flowers and vegetables grow. One way to help protect the little guys is to eliminate chemical sprays, like pesticides, which harm these important earth workers. If bees were people, they would thank you.

How sad to see litter
on our pretty planet!

Are there others like me who will
grab it and can it?

DID YOU KNOW that litterbugs
are not bugs at all?

They're PEOPLE! All kinds,
some big and some small.

Litterbugs toss trash
right down on the ground,
which gives me a frown
the whole way around.

Well Earth
Well Me
Well Me oh My oh Me!

10. Does Litter Bug You?

When playing outdoors, become a clean earth champion by picking up litter and recycling it or throwing it away. You can also turn some garbage, especially recyclables, into art or something useful. This is called *Upcycling*. Be sure to avoid picking up litter that is sharp like broken glass, and remember to wash your hands after touching rubbish!

Well Earth
Well Me
Well Me oh My oh Me!

11. Bye Bye One-Use Bottle

Try, try, try to eliminate disposable and single use items like plastic bottles. Plastic bottles leach yucky toxins into the water, and less than a third of plastic bottles actually get recycled! That's a lot of bottles that end up in landfills or that turn into pollution in our oceans. Try instead using stainless steel canteens for drinking water. It's much better for your body as well as for the earth! And then you can say, "Bye bye one-use bottle!"

I care for turtles, birds,
and all of earth's creatures.

I care for humans, too,
no matter their features!

Well Earth
Well Me
Well Me oh My oh Me!

12. Give the Critters Some Space in Their Place

One special way to help create a well earth is to leave wildlife critters undisturbed in their natural environment. Insects, birds, mammals, and sea creatures are happier when untouched by human hands. Observe them with joy and admiration, while giving them some space in their place. Enjoy nature's wonderful critters – untouched, unmoved, and thriving in their natural homes.

Well Earth
Well Me
Well Me oh My oh Me!

13. Help an Adult with a Friendly Reminder

By bringing reusable bags to the store for groceries – including for produce – you can help reduce a portion of the millions of plastic and paper bags that end up in landfills each year. Plastic bags also get blown out of landfills by the wind and cause harm to wildlife on land and in the ocean. You can offer a helpful reminder to bring the reusable bags to the store, because they're easy to forget sometimes!

Whether I live in the country
or in a big city,
on top of a mountain
or down by the sea,

I can make
the best choice,
and know that
I'm free
to use my power
to make
a well earth...
and ESPECIALLY
a very well me!

14. Celebrate Differences and Help Create a Well Earth of Peace
Children of all cultures want and need the same things: to be loved, to have fun, to learn, and to feel safe. And while children of all cultures may be the same in those four ways, it is important to honor all the unique qualities each child has as well. By respecting and celebrating each child's differences, you can actually help to create a more peaceful and well earth.

Well Earth
Well Me
Well...
little ol'
spectacular,
amazing,
wonderful,
adorable,
earth-loving,
huggable,
sun-shiny,
fabulous
ME!

15. Shine Your Brilliance

Has anyone told you lately how special and superbly, excellently wonderful you are? Well, you are hearing it right now. Use your magnificent creativity and trust your fabulously exceptional self to be empowered to make important changes for a well earth and a well you! And please share your ideas, because others will be able to learn great things from you. Let your brilliance shine!

My Pledge for a Well Earth and a Well Me!

I, _____ , will take loving care of
the earth. I will do my best to leave it a better place than how I found it.
Here is a picture of me caring for the earth:

What Readers are Saying about Well Earth Well Me!

"I believe that inspiring, empowering, and educating children in ways they can help the world and our earth is key to our future and even survival. I laud Kenda for creating a kid-friendly book with beautiful illustrations and ideas for children to help themselves and the earth."   ~Martha Nitzberg, Lead Interpretative Naturalist, Natural Bridges State Beach, CA

"If you want to teach children how to be budding environmentalists and happy citizens of the world, this is the book for you. Not only will kids love Kenda's inventive illustrations and text, she will inspire the entire family."
~Natalie Cherot, PhD, Sociologist, Publisher of Conducive Media

"*Well Earth Well Me!* received an enthusiastic "two thumbs up" from my first grade students! They absolutely loved the vivid photo illustrations and melodic rhythm of the text. This is a stunning book with a powerful message, and it sparked a wonderful conversation about how each of us, even young children, can make the world a better place."
~Lisa Boutilier, First Grade Teacher, Maryland

"I love it! It's fun, well written, nicely designed, and the pictures really add something with the thoughtful words. This is definitely a book we would use in our Religious Education program."
~Perry Montrose, R. E. Director of the Unitarian Church of Westport, Connecticut

"Kenda has captured the splendor of earth and the radiance of children in this lovely book. The ability children have to make a difference for themselves, for one another, and for healing the earth, is a clear message that can inspire all of us to take action. As a mother and founder of a national nonprofit for children, I believe **Well Earth Well Me!** offers a joyful message of coexistence. It's a treasure!"   ~Iris Rave Wedeking, Founder of Camp Kesem, California

"The photo illustrations are stunning and lively and Kenda's message is perfect for supporting young people to care for the natural world and themselves. It is a lovely resource for parents and teachers and I look forward to sharing it with the children in my life!"
~Jaime Becktel, Illustrator of My Mother is a Mountain

"I think this charming little book offers children the opportunity to recognize they are a voice and vision of hope for themselves and for planet earth."   ~Dr. Doris Arrington, A.T.R.-BC, HLM, Psychologist, Author and Educator

Words of Gratitude from Kenda

I hold heaps of gratitude in my heart to many special people who supported me with this project including my loving and lovable family and my precious community of friends. Thank you for your unending encouragement. A special thanks to: my incredible husband (whose many roles include editing, brainstorming, and all around awesome human) who stands by me with an open mind and a generous heart; my super sweet step-daughter, Jaime, who is a shining light in my life; my Mom and her enduring belief in my ability to pursue my passions; my Sistas, Tina and Elaine, who show up when I need them and who share my joys and sorrows; the Montemurno family (especially Marie, my BFF) for their editing, feedback, and unconditional love and enthusiasm; Sandy for her design expertise and for helping me articulate a vision; and Penny, who gave me this opportunity. I am eternally grateful and feel very blessed to have them all in my life. I'd like to thank all the adorable kids (some who I proudly call nephew or niece), who generously gave me permission to put images of their beautiful selves in the book: Orion, Sam, Jarod, EJ, Simon, Sophia, Samantha, Tobin, Graham, Talia, Ezra, Ava, Tess, and Meron. I'd also like to voice my gratitude to Irene Parishina for sharing that gorgeous (last) photo of Meron.

This book is dedicated to the memory of Kenneth Dale Swartz, February 28, 1936 -- June 15, 2009.

Thank you, Dad, for teaching me to respect the earth.

XO Kenda

Published by Eifrig Publishing, LLC
PO Box 66, 701 Berry Street, Lemont, PA 16851, USA
Knobelsdorffstr. 44, 14059 Berlin, Germany.

For information regarding permission, contact:
Rights and Permissions Department,
Eifrig Publishing, LLC
PO Box 66, 701 Berry Street, Lemont, PA 16851, USA.
permissions@eifrigpublishing.com, www.eifrigpublishing.com
Tel/Fax.: (888) 340-6543

Library of Congress Control Number: 2011924733

Swartz Pepper, Kenda
Well Earth Well Me!
by Kenda Swartz Pepper

p. cm.

Paperback: ISBN 978-1-936172-24-5
Hard Cover: ISBN 978-1-936172-25-2

[1. Environment- Fiction]
I. Swartz Pepper, Kenda, ill. II. Title: Well Earth Well Me!

15 14 13 12 2011
5 4 3 2 1

Book design in collaboration with Sandy Frye: www.sandyfrye.com

**Printed by Jostens in March 2011
on FSC-certified 60% PCW recycled paper. ∞**